Favorite Rag Rugs For Beginners

Many Easy Rag Rugs Projects To Décor Your Home

Copyright © 2020

All rights reserved.

DEDICATION

The author and publisher have provided this e-book to you for your personal use only. You may not make this e-book publicly available in any way. Copyright infringement is against the law. If you believe the copy of this e-book you are reading infringes on the author's copyright, please notify the publisher at: https://us.macmillan.com/piracy

Contents

WEAVE A BOHO T-SHIRT RAG RUG WITH EASY DIY LOOM..1

HOW TO MAKE BEAUTIFUL RAG RUG {& DIY T-SHIRT YARN} 23

HOW TO MAKE A DIY RUG FROM SCRATCH................45

MAKE YOUR OWN WOVEN RAG RUG...........................59

Favorite Rag Rugs For Beginners

WEAVE A BOHO T-SHIRT RAG RUG WITH EASY DIY LOOM

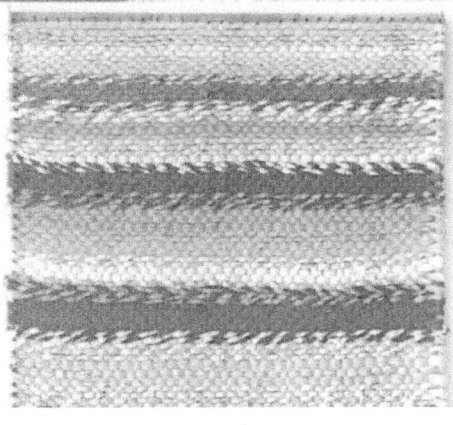

The whole process of building a simple rag rug loom and weaving a t-shirt rug was so much fun! I will share with you a couple of ways to build your own adjustable loom and some short cuts I learned on how to weave this colorful boho style T-shirt rag rug!

MATERIALS AND TOOLS TO MAKE A T-SHIRT RAG RUG AND A DIY LOOM:

To make a T-shirt rag rug, first we need to make some t-shirt yarn or any fabric yarn.

How to make t-shirt yarn and weave a round rug.

Optional but very helpful: this great rotary cutter really speeds up the t-shirt yarn making process, and here's a cutting mat to use with the cutter!

For the DIY loom, you just need a hammer, some wood, 2 wood dowels, and 2 inch flat head nails (the flat head will keep the yarn in place.

STEP 1: MAKE AN ADJUSTABLE DIY LOOM!

We made a super simple loom which you will see.

Or this one below which has a 20" by 13" weaving surface.

You can build a simple loom frame with 1x2s or other scrap wood you have, you can build them any size. Secure the four corners with dowels so the frame is adjustable length-wise. See plan below-

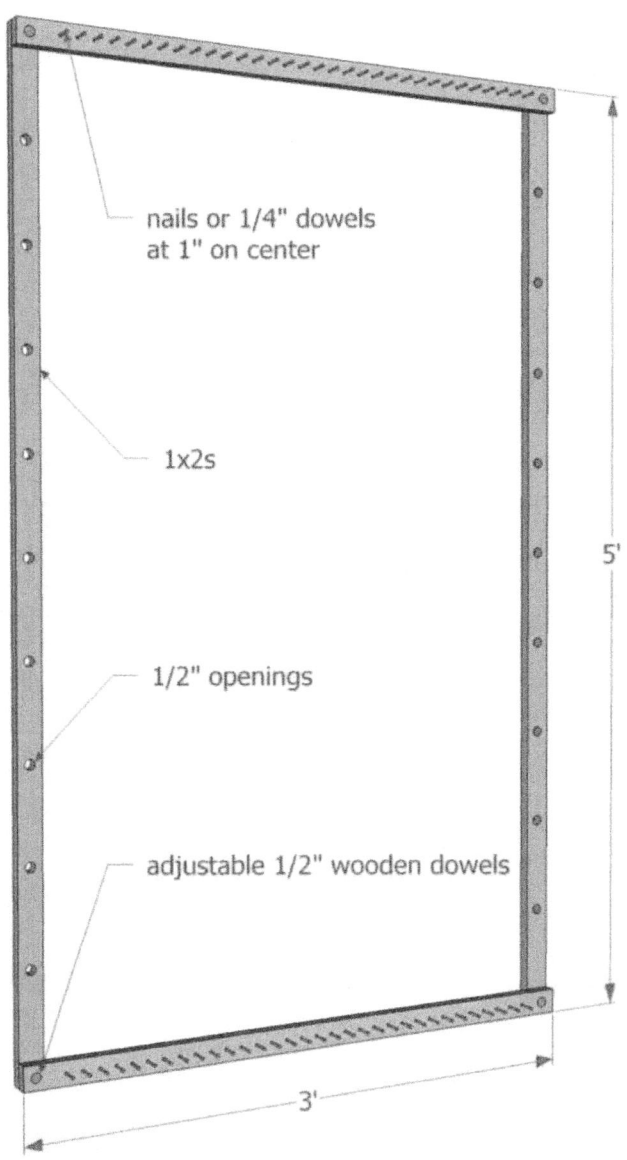

You can build a stand for this loom, or just hang it on the wall.

We did it in a even more simplified way. Instead of building the whole frame, we only set up the top and bottom bars, and screwed them into the wall. (If you don't want holes in your wall, then build the whole frame like shown in the plan!) The nails are spaced at 1" apart.

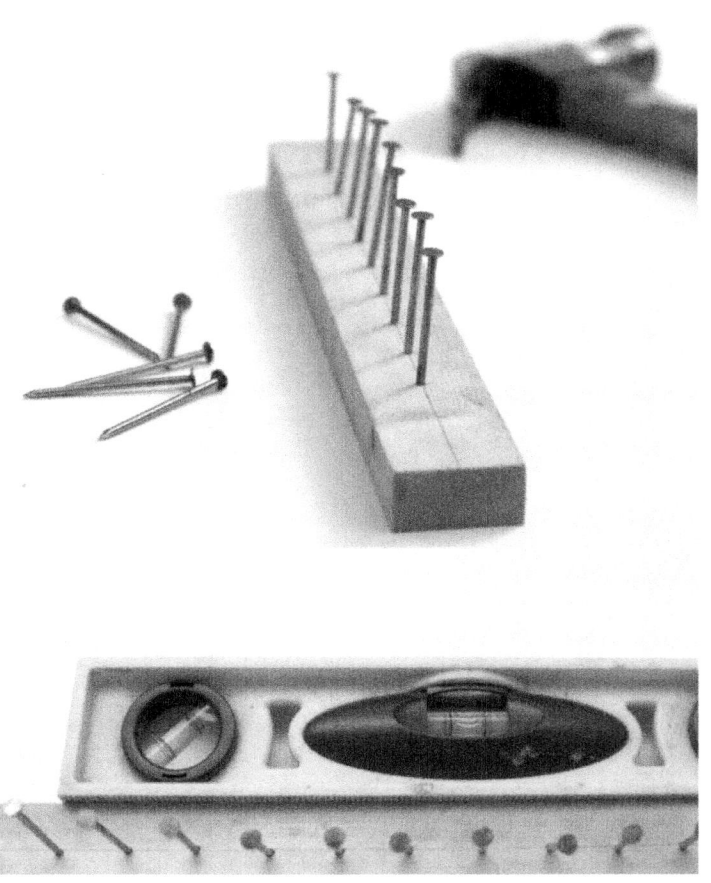

It is also important to add two 1/2" to 3/4" diameter wood or metal dowels, one on each side of the loom, see photo and description in next step below.

STEP 2: START WEAVING THE RUG WITH CONTINUOUS WARP.

REMEMBER THESE TWO WORDS: WARP & WEFT.

Warp: in weaving, the threads on a loom (the pink yarn threads shown here) over and under which other threads (the Weft, in this case our colorful t-shirt yarn) are passed to make textile.

You can use string or t-shirt yarn as warp. I used some acrylic yarn.

Tie a loop at the very beginning. Zigzag the warp onto the nails on the upper and lower bars. Tie a loop at the end.

The warp should not be stretched too tight. As we weave, they will become tighter.

In addition to the frame, you will also need two side "bars" to help the rug stay rectangular as we weave, because the tension will pull the shape towards the center.

I used a piece of quarter round trim piece on each side. Thin metals rods or 1/2" to 1/4" wood dowels are popular choices also. Tie a string to secure ends of these bars onto the end nails / screws . We will need to be able to remove the from the rug at the end. See following steps.

I found the tension to be quite strong that the wood trim pieces stated warping. So I added 1-2 extra nails to help them stay straight.

STEP 3: DOUBLE WEFT RUG WEAVING

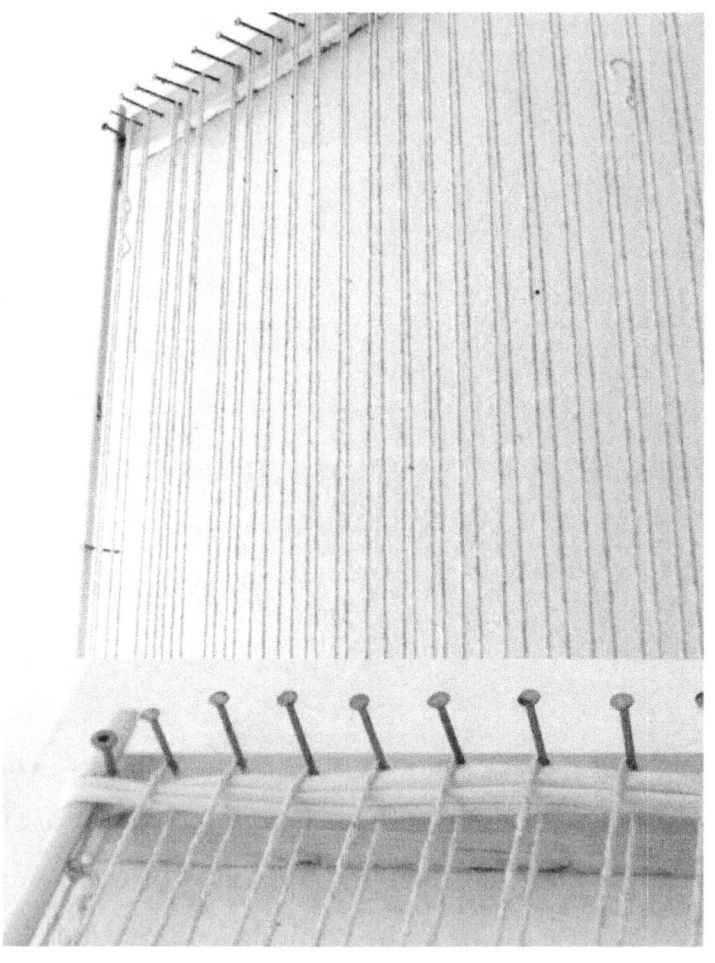

Take a piece of t-shirt yarn, fold in the middle so you have a double strand.

Go through the first loop we tied on the warp like shown above. This is the only tricky part. You can also stitch this spot, or tie a knot- the goal is to prevent the t-shirt rag rug from unraveling at this beginning spot.

Now take the doubled weft and weave it over and under the warp.

Favorite Rag Rugs For Beginners

In case you missed the definitions – Warp: (in weaving) the threads on a loom over and under which other threads (the Weft) are passed to make textile.

When you reach the end, turn the corner and weave the weft over and under the warp, alternating from the row above.

That's the basics. Next we will look at how to change colors and create designs in our t-shirt rag rug!

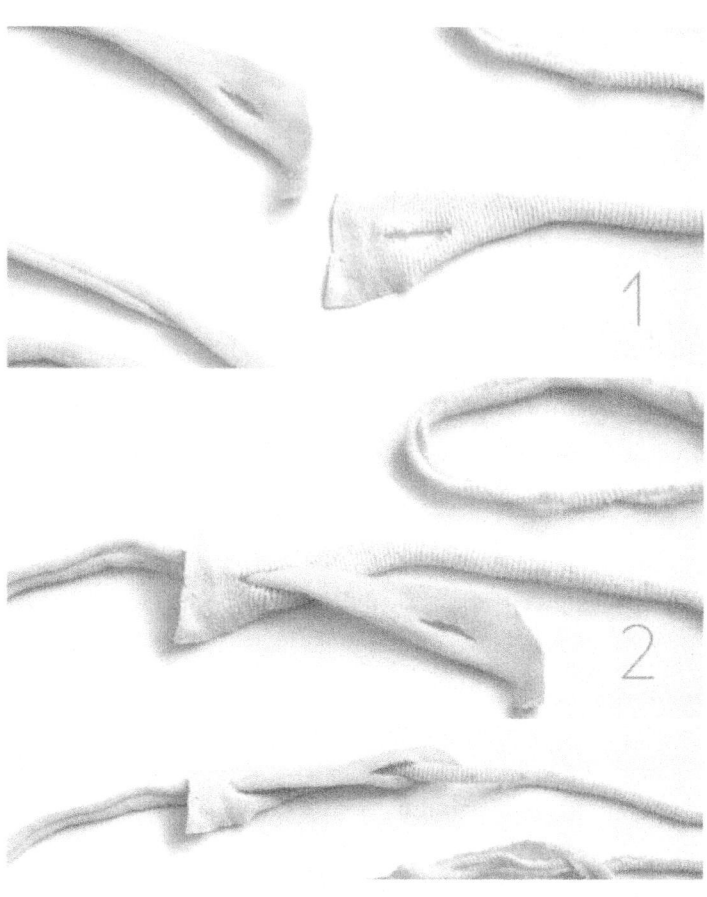

Because I was weaving with double strands, it was fun to play with combinations of colors.

As you can see, I changed the colors from yellow-yellow, to yellow-white, to white-white, etc. The possibilities are endless!

When using two colors, you can create a "peppermint" look by twisting the two color strands as you weave.

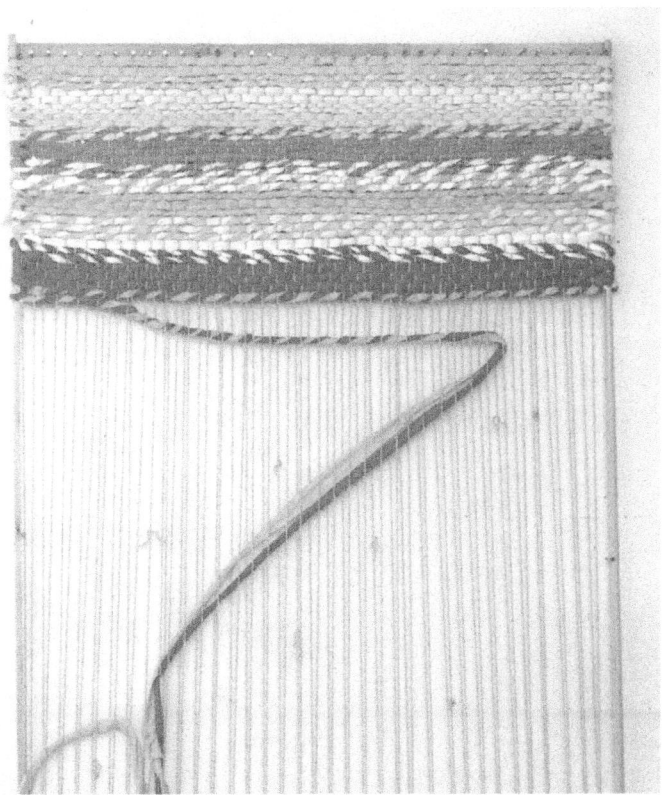

Push each row up as you weave. The rug will stay nice and tight, and you can take a break and come back to it anytime!

Once you reach the desired length on the t-shirt rag rug, remove the warp one section at a time from the bottom bar. Tie a knot as you remove each piece. Slide out the side bars from the rug.

Trim the warp at where we tied the knots. If you weave all the way to the bottom bar, you may not have any extra warp to trim.

HOW TO MAKE BEAUTIFUL RAG RUG {& DIY T-SHIRT YARN}

MATERIALS AND TOOLS TO MAKE A RAG RUG FROM T-SHIRT YARN:

old T-shirts: field trip to Salvation Army, woohoo! I chose mostly cotton, but other fabrics will work too. To weave a 30" diameter rug, we need about 6-7 x-large (women's) t-shirts.

hula hoop or cardboard: I started with cardboard because as a total newbie, I was just going to do a quick test first. But I loved the "test" so much that I transferred it to a bigger 30" diameter hula hoop! You will see more details about both methods!

scissors

STEP 1: CHOOSING FABRIC COLORS FOR YOUR DIY RAG RUG

How much fabric do I need to make t-shirt yarn? To weave a 30" diameter rug, we need about 6-7 x-large (women's) t-shirts.

On my first trip to Salvation Army to get fabrics to make our rag rug, I ended up with a pile of t-shirts the size of an elephant… Realizing I was totally lost in all the colors, I put them all back!

See, colors are like musical notes, the more isn't the better. It's really about harmony!

After a color study using my favorite colors – hot pink, yellow, and blue-turquoise, I returned to Salvation Army with a list of colors, much more focus, and great efficiency! ☺

STEP 2: HOW TO MAKE CONTINUOUS T-SHIRT YARN FOR WEAVING A RAG RUG

IMPORTANT: keep the yarn in shorter lengths in this step, and organized the same color piece into a "yarn ball". If the length is too long it would be hard to weave them through in next step.

The trick here is to adjust the width of your t-shirt strips: cut the strips wider for thin fabrics, narrower for thick fabrics, so the finished t-shirt yarn stays at a consistent thickness.

For most common t-shirts, 1.5" to 2" wide t-shirt strips works great for t-shirt yarn. Follow the diagram below, first cut off the sleeves and open up the t-shirt.

Then cut the lines cross the body, you can use this great rotary cutter which really speeds up the t-shirt yarn making process, on a cutting mat, or use scissors.

Because the fabric stretches in the direction of the cut, we can pull it to form curled fabric yarn, as in the photo below.

Roll pieces of each color t-shirt yarn into a ball for use later.

IMPORTANT: keep the yarn in shorter lengths in this step, and organized the same color piece into a "yarn ball".

STEP 3: MAKE A CARDBOARD LOOM, OR HULA HOOP LOOM

If you don't have a hula hoop, you can make a rug on a cardboard loom of any size by joining several pieces of cardboard together with glue and tape.

I started small as a test, so I ended up using both types of looms, you can skip the cardboard and just use the hula hoop for bigger rugs! =)

To make a cardboard loom, first draw a big circle using a circular object as a guide. Divide the circle into equal parts, here I used a protractor and divided the circle into 10 degree segments.

Cut the circle but leave 1" to 2" of cardboard around the circle, make slits so the yarn can be held in place as shown in #3 and #4. If you start with a hula hoop as loom, you will need some tape or clips to secure the yarn at the beginning, so it does not shift too much.

STEP 4: WEAVING THE RAG RUG

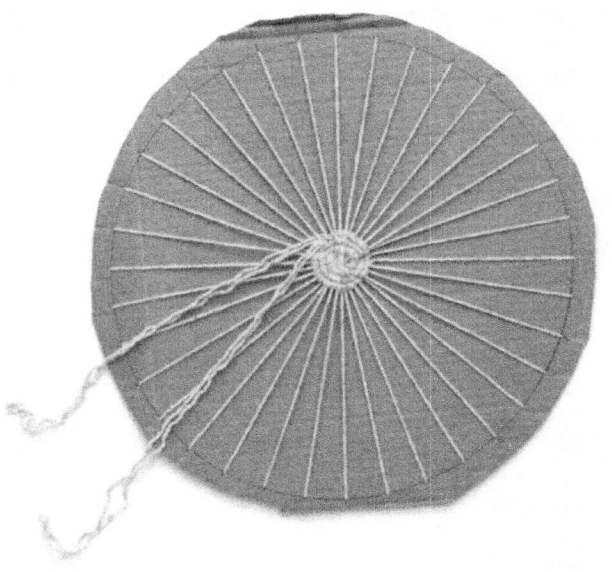

I started with some scrap yarn then covered it with a yellow pompom (more on pompoms later). You can also start with t-shirt yarn and use narrower strips for the beginning.

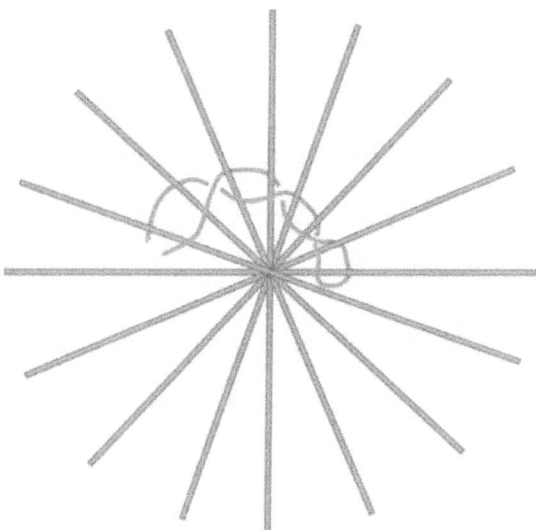

Choose a direction, either clockwise or counter clockwise, weave over and under every two weft (the crosswise yarns) for the first few rounds, then every weft for the rest.

When I transferred the piece (started the cardboard) to the hula hoop, I just extended the yarn, and doubled each thread which is optional.

You can remove the cardboard at any time in the phase. As I mentioned earlier, you can start from the beginning on a hula hoop loom and skip the cardboard loom. (Remember I was testing on cardboard, and later decided to make a larger rug?) Continue to add t-shirt yarn, connect them as shown in step #1.

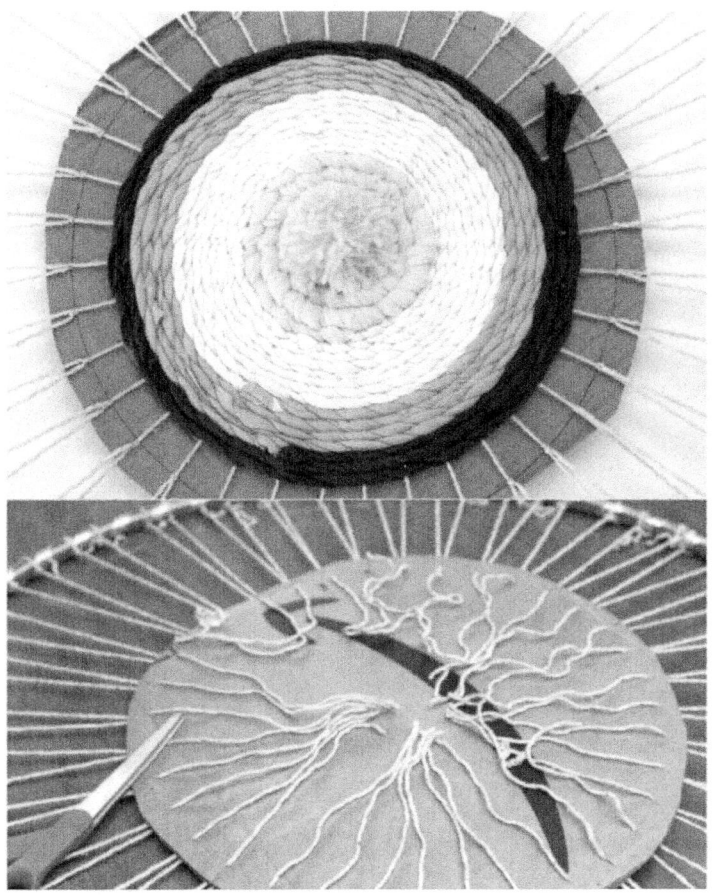

Try to complete each color t-shirt yarn as whole circles, this will help keep a circular shape as we weave.

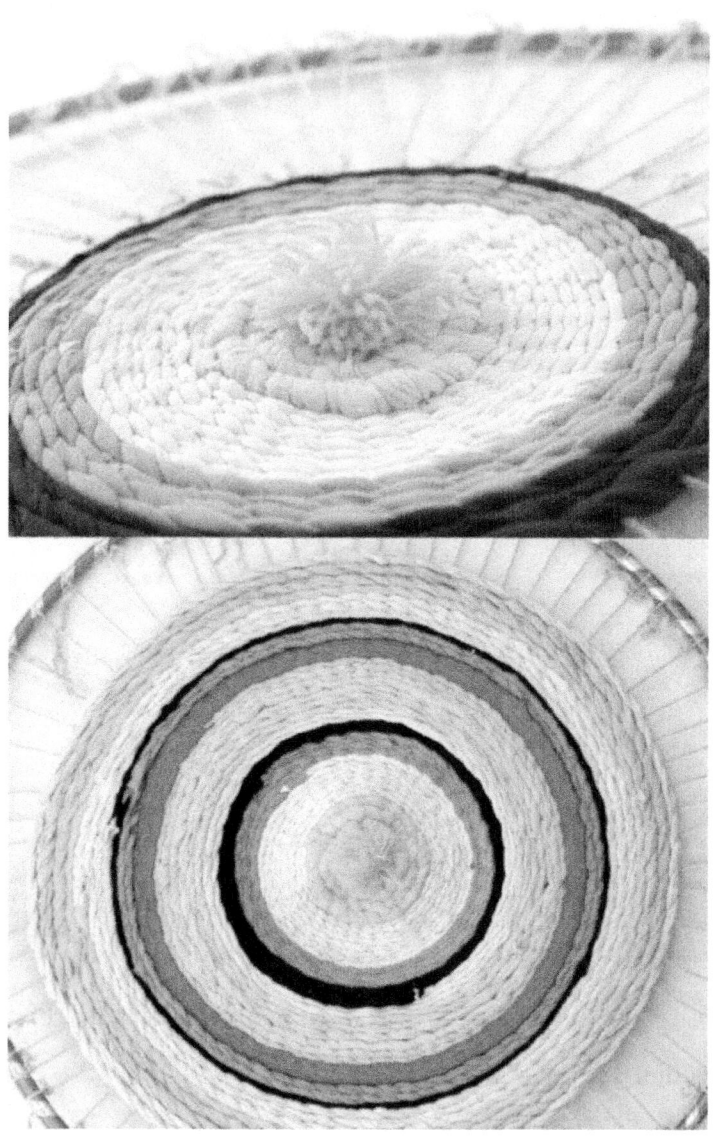

STEP 5: FINISHING TOUCHES

Once we get to the end of the last circle of weave, just tie a knot or stitch the last two ends to stop any unraveling. Cut the weft and tie a secure knot with every two pieces.

The outer edge may seem like it's curling up. No worries, once all the knots are tied, it will stay flat again.

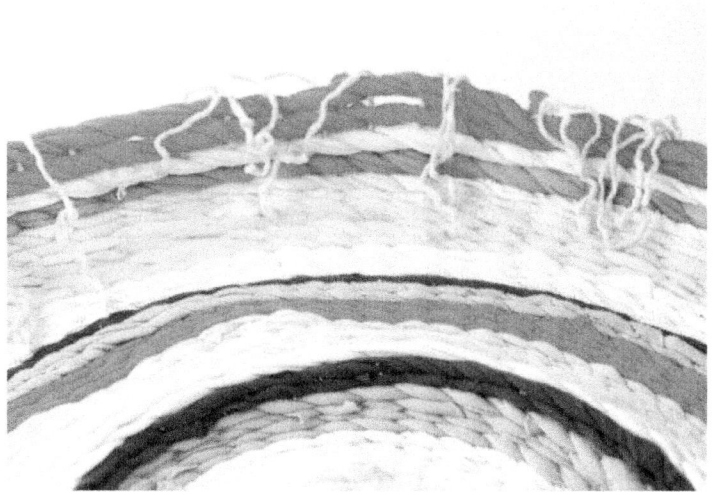

Make some tassels by splitting the ends of a piece of yarn and tie a knot in the center with 1 or 2 pieces.

The pompoms are made with thin strips of t-shirt yarn. Here's a tutorial on how to make pom poms super fast in big batches!

To attach the pompoms and tassels, just tie them through any part of the rug, they will be easy to replace too.

HOW TO MAKE A DIY RUG FROM SCRATCH

This DIY rug technique can be used for a runner, a small rug in the kitchen or bathroom, or even a larger rug for seating areas like mine. Want to make your own cotton rug like this one?

Here are the step by step instructions…

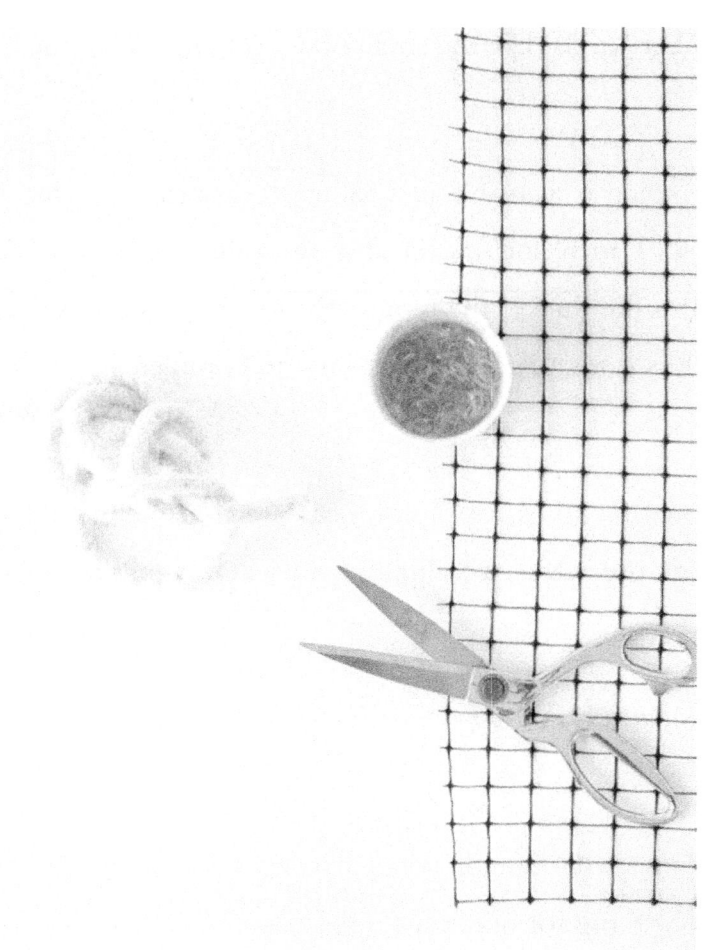

How to Make a DIY Rug with Cotton Piping

DIY Rug Materials

Multi-use netting

Cotton piping*

Small rubber bands (like the small ones you can find in the hair aisle)

Scissors

*Cotton piping is available in various thicknesses (ranging from 1/4 inch up to 1 inch and more) and any thickness will work for this project. But the thicker the piping, the faster the DIY process will be (and the less yards you will need to use to complete it).

My personal favorites for piping sizes are: 1/2 inch and 11/16 inch, but you can use ANY size. Piping comes in lots of sizes.

How to Make a DIY Rug – Step by Step Instructions

1. Determine what length you'd like your rug to be. In my case, I wanted a 5×8 rug for underneath the couch.

My roll of netting is smaller than that, so I did some quick math to determine how many pieces I would need to cut to make a 5X8 rug (3 pieces that are 8 feet long, since the netting is 2 feet wide). And I would have an extra foot leftover from the width, that I could cut off of the mesh before getting started, etc.

Once you have that figured out, roll out the length of the netting you need and cut the pieces with a pair of scissors.

2. Next, start cutting pieces of cotton piping that are about 4 inches long (each). You want them all to be roughly the same length, so that the rug looks relatively even when its completed, while also having a little bit of variation, so you can more of a textured feel that looks handmade (and not manufactured).

Note: Depending on the size of your rug, you're going to need a lot more cotton piping than you might expect. To give you a better idea of what I'm talking about…we used more than 200 yards of cotton piping for an 5×8 rug. That's a lot of cotton!

But cotton piping is pretty affordable, so it's still relatively budget-friendly, when you consider the cost of a thick handmade rug like this one would cost thousands of dollars to purchase in store. The cost of materials for a 5×8 rug totaled $300-350.

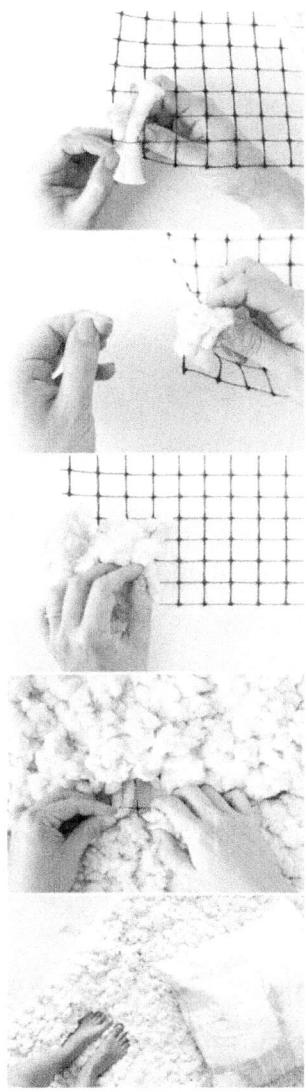

3. Next, weave the cut cotton pieces in between the netting grid, as shown in the photo. Then, pull the pieces upward and tie them together with a rubber band (again, as shown in the photo).

Once secured with a rubber band, fluff out the piping pieces so they have more of a fuzzy pom-pom shape.

4. Repeat steps #2 and #3 until you've completely covered the netting pieces you cut in step #1.

5. Now it's time to assemble the pieces into one single unit. This may not apply if you're making a small rug or a runner.

The process is the pretty much the same as step #3, but this time, you'll be weaving pieces though the ends of each separate piece of mesh to bring them together as one.

Securing them together in the 'pom-pom form' (for lack of a better term) with rubber bands, and fluffing them out once secure.

6. Repeat this process along the edge of all pieces that need to be joined together until completed.

7. Lastly, trim any edge or interior pieces that feel like they need it, with a pair of sharp sicissors.

I like to trim the outer edges all the way around to make them even to one another and then occasionally, there will be an interior pieces that needs a trim because it's way longer than the others.

Steps that sow to make a large-scale rug from scratch with cotton piping and a few other supplies.

Update: Note about Cotton Piping Sizes

You can use any size piping to create a rug like the ones you see in this post, but one thing to note in that the smaller the piping, the more it will take to complete your rug.

So for example, if you use a cotton piping that is 1/6 inch thick, you may need to double that piping up in the netting to get a thick, cushy look like mine. But if you use piping that is a 1/2 inch or thicker, you will not need to do that.

My favorite cotton piping sizes for the rugs I've made with this technique are 1/2 inch and 11/16 inch. I also like 1 inch thick piping, but not quite as much as the other two.

This is just what I like though. You may find a groove with a different size that you like better, so it doesn't hurt to buy a very small amount (like a couple of feet) of a few different sizes to test them out first before buying lots of yardage. You can find cotton piping by the yard at craft supply stores like JoAnn's, usually with the upholstery supplies.

Update: Note About Using Rubber Bands to Secure the Piping

It is true that over time (years) rubber bands may deteriorate or break. This was not an issue for me personally, but there are many comments asking questions about this particular thing. So, if you would prefer not to use rubber bands, there is another option.

Pull each one tight and double knot it then cut off the excess. NOTE: This will be more time consuming than the rubber band method. And for me, the rubber bands have held up quite well. But I wanted to share this option for anyone that would prefer to use something else.

I'll be the first to admit, the process is time-consuming. I'm not going to lie. BUT the results are really pretty cool, if you ask me.

And literally ANYONE at any skill level can make one, as long as you have the patience to stick it out. And then you can add rug making to your list of skills!

The process is SUPER easy. It'd be a good nightly ritual while sitting down to watch a movie, etc. Kind of like knitting…slowly plugging away at a project a couple of hours a night until it's done.

And when it's done, you have an actual rug to show for it. That you made yourself! How many people can say that that they made a rug?!

How to Care for your DIY Rug

I recommend spot cleaning for spills. Since you are using a cotton material, any spot cleaner that would work on this material should be fine. Just dab the area clean / dry when finished, instead of rubbing.

For spills and stains that aren't able to be spot cleaned and are in need of repair, the piping can be removed and replaced with new piping very easily.

Just remove the piping that is damaged or stained beyond repair and use the same method you used initially to fill in the missing pieces.

Does this Area Rug Shed?

The rug does shed a little at first, just as many other rugs this still do. But it sheds less and less as time goes on.

Is this Rug Technique Similar to Latch Hook?

It is kind of similar, but there are two key differences. One of those difference is that the cotton cording I used to create this DIY rug isn't secured on it's own (with a knot like latch hook is). And the second key difference is that there are no special tools to use.

As you can see in the materials list toward the top of this post, there aren't very many materials or special supplies need to create this rug. Which in my opinion, is a huge plus. No learning curve for new tools required!

So, there really is no limit on the size for this project – big or small.

MAKE YOUR OWN WOVEN RAG RUG

I've certainly done my fair share of DIY projects through the years, but for all the projects I have completed thus far, I've yet to venture into the land of rugs—until today! I wanted to make a kitchen rug for the studio that was: a) cute, b) woven, and c) relatively easy for a first time rug maker. After a bit of research, I found the perfect woven rug that fits all my needs! If you have a few old bedsheets around, this is the perfect way to use them (and get an adorable rug out of the process).

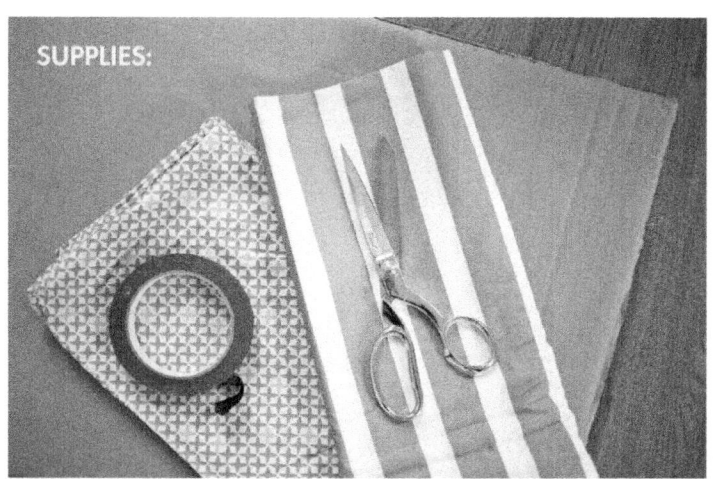

Supplies:

-3 king size, flat, cotton bedsheets

-piece of cardboard, 23" x 43"

-fabric scissors

-masking tape

-marker

-ruler

Step One: Use your ruler and marker to make a mark every 2" across the longest side of each of your bedsheets.

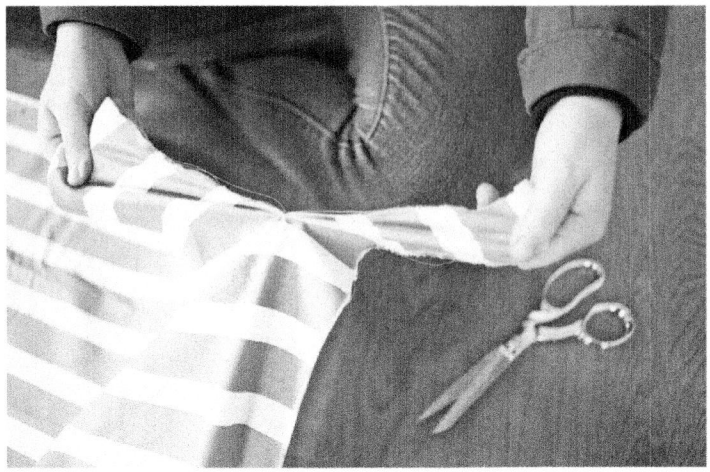

Use fabric scissors to make a 2" cut at each mark.

Step Two: At each cut, rip the fabric apart, and it should tear evenly all the way across the sheet. Repeat process until each sheet is ripped into even strips. Separate strips by color and pattern.

Step Three: On each of the short ends of your cardboard, start 2" from each end and mark 2" long lines every 1/2". Use scissors to cut 2" slots at each mark.

Step Four: Gather three fabric strips of various colors into a group, fold the group in half lengthwise, and place one end into the first slot (it should hang over the edge a few inches).

Place the other end into the corresponding spot on the opposite side.

If you have a lot of strings hanging off the sides of your strips, try and pull the big clumps of strings off before you place into the cardboard slots. Repeat this process for each strip across the cardboard. It will get pretty full after you have a few groups placed, but just keep going until you are done.

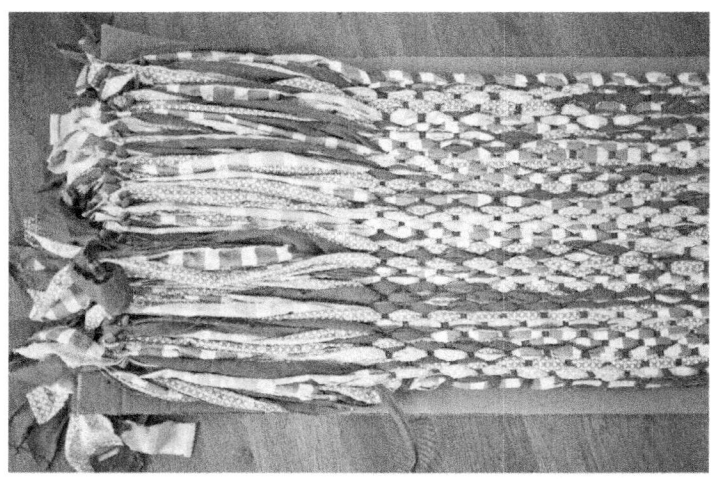

Step Five: Designate one color as your weaving strip, and wrap a piece of masking tape around one end to make it easier to weave through the strips. Starting about 2" in from the end of your cardboard slots, begin to weave the weaving strip under and over each group until you get to the other side. Make sure to leave a 6" tail at your beginning spot (you'll lengthen this at the end). Because the cardboard is so full, the first row of weaving will be the hardest since it's difficult to tell one group from another. Just do the best you can, and if you get a few strips into the wrong bunch, it won't make a difference at the end.

Once you get to the other end with your weaving strip, make a U-turn by going over or under the last bunch (whichever is needed depending on where you end up), and weave your way back to the other side (it should be much easier this time). As you finish each row, straighten out the weaved strip with your fingers and slide it as close to the row before it as you can. Repeat the weaving process until you are about 2" from the cardboard slots on the other end of the rug. Make sure to pay attention to the width of your rug as you go, and keep it as even as you can. This type of weaving gives you a lot of control over your width since you can simply tighten or loosen your strip as you make the turn at each end.

When you get to the end of your weaving strip, you'll want to join a new strip to the existing one so you can keep on weaving. Cut a slot into the end of your weaving strip and the beginning of your new strip. Pull an inch or two of your new strip through the slot on the existing strip. Pass the tail end of your new strip through the slot on the new strip, and pull tight. Now you have a longer strip! Keep doing that each time you need to extend your weaving strip.

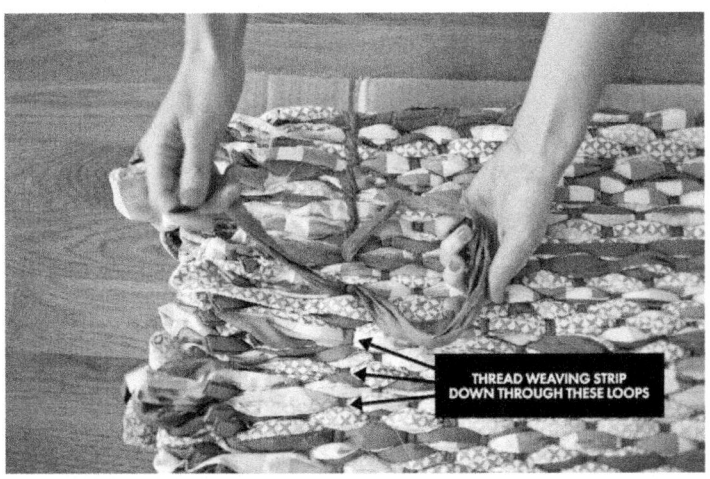

Step Six: To finish the ends, make a U-turn around the last bunch where your weaving ended, and thread your weaving strip down through the first exposed section of your last row of weaving (see above photo). Pull tight. Again, cross over to the next exposed weaving and thread down through that section and pull tight. Continue until you reach the end, and tie your weaving strip onto one of the strips in the last group of strips. Repeat process on the opposite end (you'll have to join a strip to lengthen the tail of your beginning weaving strip first).

Step Seven: You're almost done! Just place a ruler or a piece of cardboard inside of where you want to trim your ends and use fabric scissors to trim the excess pieces. Once the ends are cut, you can remove the cardboard backing. You did it! You just made a rug!

Printed in Dunstable, United Kingdom